Charleston
South Carolina
AND THE LOWCOUNTRY

A PHOTOGRAPHIC PORTRAIT

First published in the United States
of America by:

Twin Lights Publishers, Inc.
10 Hale Street
Rockport, Massachusetts 01966
Telephone: (978) 546-7398
http://www.twinlightspub.com

and

Yourtown Books
Naples, Florida
Telephone: (941) 262-0716

ISBN 1-885435-35-5

10 9 8 7 6 5 4 3 2

Book design by
SYP Design & Production, Inc.
http://www.sypdesign.com

Cover Photo by: E. B. Heston
Back Cover Photos by: James Blank,
Debra Gingrich, and E. B. Heston

Printed in China

Other titles in the Photographic Portrait series:

Cape Ann
Kittery to the Kennebunks
The Mystic Coast, Stonington to New London
The White Mountains
Boston's South Shore
Upper Cape Cod
The Rhode Island Coast
Greater Newburyport
Portsmouth and Coastal New Hampshire
Naples, Florida
Sarasota, Florida
The British Virgin Islands
Portland, Maine
Mid and Lower Cape Cod
The Berkshires
Boston
Camden, Maine
Sanibel and Captiva Islands
San Diego's North County Coast
Newport Beach, California
Phoenix and the Valley of the Sun
Wasatch Mountains, Utah
The Florida Keys
Miami and South Beach
Maryland's Eastern Shore
Asheville, North Carolina
Savannah, Georgia

ACKNOWLEDGMENTS

Twin Lights Publishers and Yourtown Books wish to
thank all of the photographers who submitted their work
for our consideration. Because of space limitations, we
were not able to include many excellent photographs in
*Charleston, South Carolina and the Lowcountry: A
Photographic Portrait.*

We extend our thanks to the people at The Charleston
City Paper (www.charlestoncitypaper.com) and Ritz
Camera (www.ritzcamera.com) for judging the contest.
Their expertise has resulted in three winning photographs,
as well as a selection of photographs that describe the
Charleston area beautifully.

We are grateful to Sarah FK Coble, who wrote the cap-
tions for the photographs. A nationally published free-
lance writer, she is a contributor to *Miami and South
Beach: A Photographic Portrait, Florida International
Magazine, Naples Illustrated,* and the *Naples Literary
Review.* Her work has been published in the *Sanibel
Captiva Review, Gulfshore Life, Gulfshore Style,* and *Home
and Condo* magazines.

Special thanks go to E.B. Heston of Palmetto Carriage
Works, Ltd. for sharing his intimate knowledge of the
city and its history. Debra Gingrinch of Carolina
Helicopter Services for the use of her aerial photographs,
Patriot Point Naval and Maritime Museum
(www.state.sc.us/patpt/), The Citadel–The Military
College of the South (www.citadel.edu), and the
Charleston Area Convention and Visitors Bureau
(www.charlestoncvb.com), for the use of their courtesy
photographs. All of the photo and camera shops in the
Charleston area that helped host the contest.

Finally, our thanks to Sara Day who has created another
beautiful book.

CONTENTS

Introduction

4

North to Isle of Palms

13

Historic Downtown

42

South to Kiawah Island

97

Introduction

Charleston is a city apart; a world unto itself.

Since its very founding as a colony in the 17th century, Charleston has been a unique American treasure, blending the principled idealism with which it was founded with the hard-headed pragmatism which kept it alive; soft-spoken country life with well-bred urbanity; and a solid sense of its own history with a discerning eye for progress.

Seated serenely on the coast, buffered from the Atlantic by wild, sandy barrier islands and held in the cradle of the Carolina Lowcountry, Charleston is defined by its geography. The Carolina Lowcountry is indeed low: a rough triangle of land that serves as the watershed for the mist-covered Appalachian mountains to the northwest, the country is swampy, marshy, and mysterious. While rivers cascade down from the hills and carve out the islands and the land on which Charleston sits, the sea drifts against the city's venerable batteries. The natural boundaries of river and sea and swamp has effectively isolated and restrained Charleston from the sprawl that seems to have engulfed the rest of the country. The old city maintains a powerful and vibrant presence in the lives of modern Charlestonians.

Yet for all its isolation, Charleston has always been fertile ground for the grand experiments that is part of the American Saga. It was home to the first revolutionaries and statesmen and it was there that a Provincial Congress assembled and signed a constitution establishing the first independent government in America. It was also in Charleston that secession was first proclaimed and state's rights were fiercely defended in the war between the states. Yet, Charleston is still regarded as America's most polite city; a cultural capital of Southern hospitality and charm. Time and again, its waterfront battery and urban streets have been blown by hurricanes, ravaged by fire, and shaken by earthquakes and artillery shells, yet they are still graced with beautifully preserved and much loved historic buildings and ancient moss draped trees.

In spite of the careful preservation of its history, Charleston has also been a progressive bastion for the performing and visual arts. It is home to a widely acclaimed symphony, the Gibbes Museum of Art and countless art galleries, numerous dance and theater companies, as well as the world renown Spoleto and Piccolo Spoleto festivals of the performing arts.

Charleston, South Carolina and the Lowcountry: A Photographic Portrait, unveils a whole new view of the many facets of one of the loveliest gems in the American treasury.

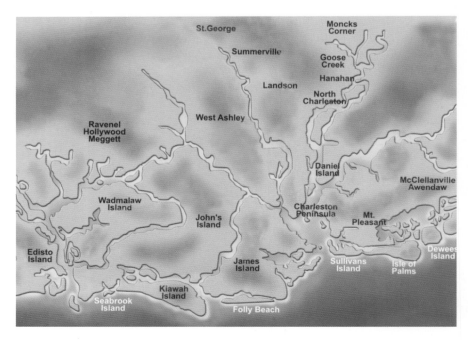

Morris Island Lighthouse

WILLIAM PALMER
NIKON N90S
FUJI VELVIA

A solitary beacon, this lighthouse stands as the only structure on the strand of Morris Island. The now uninhabited island was the site of the bitter and poignant battle between Confederate defenders and Union forces, spearheaded by the black soldiers of the celebrated 54th Massachusetts Regiment for Battery Wagner, a lightly defended fort on the south entrance of Charleston Harbor.

It was William "Buff" Palmer's intense interest in nature photography that led him to the Carolina Lowcountry. An American born in Venezuela and raised in Puerto Rico, Palmer moved to the U.S. at 16, then began his studies in photo-journalism at Indiana University. After extensive travel in America and Europe, Palmer made his home in Charleston, pursuing his passion for photographing the natural beauty of the Lowcountry. His image of Morris Island Lighthouse, taken from the old coast guard station on Folly Beach is a singularly romantic perspective of this historic monument. "The fact that this is one of the last undeveloped beaches in the area makes this location a particular favorite," he writes. "I was out bird watching in the woods when I turned around and saw this incredible view of the lighthouse. It was calling my name. I'm always listening and looking for that 'moment' in time that brings out the true heart of the natural beauty that surrounds us."

Pond at Middleton Place

JAMES BLANK
PENTAX 67
EKTACHROME 64
F22

Middleton Place was part of Mary Williams'
dowry for her marriage to Henry Middleton
in 1741. The rolling property sits on high
ground, above the floodplain of the Ashley
River, making it a particularly desirable
property. It is said that 100 slaves were
needed to create the magnificently serene
gardens, ponds, and terraces.

"This image of the pond at Middleton Place was taken on a steamy summer day some years
ago, although my favorite time of year to photograph Charleston is early spring when there
are so many flowers and the temperature is just right," writes photographer James Blank
from his home in Chula Vista, California. A professional photographer since the age of fif-
teen, Blank's love of photographing landscapes compelled him to traverse the U.S. and
Canada capturing North America's most scenic cities and countryside on film. His work
can be seen in numerous magazines, travel books, calendars, postcards, and posters.

Historic Viewpoint
The Bells of St. Michael's

E. B. HESTON
HASSEL BLAD
AGFA VELVIA
F22

The ringing of the bells in the steeple of St. Michael's is a much loved tradition of Charleston. They are, in fact, an audible reminder of Charleston's history of faith and graceful persistence in times of trial. They rang in defiance of the British Crown in 1765, and of the Union defeat of the city in 1865. In 1993, they were recast in Britain as part of the St. Michael's restoration project and rang again in a special, daylong ceremony on July 4th to celebrate their homecoming.

Driving the cobbled streets behind two of his mules, Hoot and Tom, Charleston tour guide for Palmetto Carriage Works Ltd., photographer, and postcard publisher, E.B. Heston, has gotten to know all the ins and outs and nooks and crannies of his adopted city. "From the carriage, this view was particularly striking in the early morning light," he explains of his image of St. Michael's alabaster spire. "It's a historical view," he adds. "There are no utility lines, no telephone poles—it is the same view as someone from the 19th century would have had." Formerly a newspaper production manager in Columbus, Ohio, Heston embraced Charleston as his new home because "The sun shines every day in Charleston."

North to Isle of Palms

Tidal Marsh, Shem Creek

E. B. HESTON
HASSEL BLAD
AGFA VELVIA
F22

Tidal marshes winding worlds of grassy creeks and inlets are ubiquitous features of the Lowcountry landscape. These marshes, which fill and empty with the constant rhythm of the tides are home to a wide variety of aquatic and bird life.

Lotus Blooms on the Edge
of a Freshwater Swamp *(above)*

ALLENE C. BARANS
CANON ELAN
KODAK
F11

In the lush swamps of the Carolina Lowcountry, gold blooms.

Deer in Wildflowers *(left)*

JULIE G. ROWE
MINOLTA MAXXUM XTSI
KODAK ELITECHROME 100 SLIDE FILM

A deer stands in a meadow at Boone Hall plantation. Originally covering 17,000 acres and owned by the Boone family from 1700 to 1817, Boone Hall plantation's remaining 738 acres still grow commercial crops as well as fields of wildflowers.

Live Oak Avenue, Boone Hall Plantation *(opposite)*

JULIE G. ROWE
MINOLTA MAXXUM XTSI
KODAK ELITECHROME 100 SLIDE FILM

The dramatic, half-mile long Avenue of Oaks was planted by Captain Thomas Boone in the 18th century. Captain Thomas Boone, the planter of the Avenue's first trees, is buried midway down the Avenue, under the moss-garlanded trees.

The Bridge Over Shem Creek at Dusk *(above)*

SUSAN P. SHAMOUN
MINOLTA X-700
KODAK 100 ELITE CHROME
F4

The masts of commercial shrimping boats spike the skyline over Shem's Creek. In 1929, the bridge spanning the Cooper River joined the area of Mount Pleasant with the Charleston peninsula, making picturesque Shem Creek a popular visitor spot.

Christmas, West Ashley *(left)*

CRAIG M. LLOYD
CANON
POLAROID 35MM
F5.6

A holiday light display dazzles the eye on a balmy South Carolina December night.

Pecan Tree, Boone Hall Plantation

JULIE G. ROWE
MINOLTA MAXXUM XTSI
KODAK 100 SLIDE FILM

Pecan trees at Boone Hall were planted in 1904. It was then the largest pecan grove in the world.

Shem Creek *(top)*

CHARLESTON AREA CONVENTION
AND VISITORS BUREAU

Fish and shrimp are integral ingredients in the life and kitchens of
Charleston and the Lowcountry. Shrimp trawlers bob in the reedy
waters of Shem Creek.

Gulls on the Rigging *(bottom)*

ALLENE C. BARANS
CANON ELAN
KODAK
F11

Sea gulls wait their portion of the catch of the day on the rigging
of a trawler.

Shrimp Boat at Sunset

DONNA HUFFMAN
NIKON 2020
EKTACHROME

With the Atlantic Ocean as its front door, ocean commerce, from shrimping to piracy, has shaped Charleston's unique economic history.

Carolina Gold

ALLENE C. BARANS
CANON ELAN
KODAK
F11

Carolina Lowcountry's lush wetlands invited the cultivation of rice,
indigo and cotton, side by side with beautiful ornamental flowers.

Bridge at Magnolia Plantation

JAMES BLANK
LINHOF TECHNIKA 4X5
EKTACHROME 64
F45

Magnolia Plantation was originally the family seat of the Drayton
family, a plantation family from Barbados. The extravagantly romantic
gardens were built by Reverend Grimke-Drayton from 1843-1870 to
comfort his homesick wife.

Middleton Place *(opposite)*

JAMES BLANK
PENTAX 67
EKTACHROME 64
F16

Nestled on the banks of the Ashley River, Middleton Place's classical gardens were developed from the early to mid 18th century.

Cypress Gardens *(left)*

SOPHIE HELTAI
OLYMPUS SUPER 200N
KODAK 35MM
AUTO FLASH

Cypress Gardens, a 162-acre blackwater cypress swamp, was once part of Dean Hall, a large rice plantation built in 1775.

Dunes West, Mount Pleasant

P. L. TOMPKINS
MINOLTA SLR
35 MAX 400
AUTO

The very first golf course in America was laid out in Charleston in 1786. Since then, Charlestonians take some considerable pride in the wealth of world-ranked courses. The highly rated Dunes West, designed by Arthur Hills on the site of the historic Lexington Plantation, offers golfers the full beauty of its Lowcountry setting.

Boone Hall Plantation *(above)*

JAMES BLANK
PENTAX 67
EKTACHROME 64
F16

The earlier plantation house of Boone Hall Plantation was replaced by this brick, Georgian style mansion in 1935. Cooper River gray bricks, which were manufactured on the plantation, were well-known in the region and were used to build the walls, paths, outbuildings as well as the current main house.

Avenue of Oaks *(opposite)*

JAMES BLANK
PENTAX 67
EKTACHROME 64
F16

The majestic "Avenue of Oaks" at Boone Hall Plantation, together with the plantation's "Slave Street," of unusual brick slave cabins and a smokehouse, is listed on the Register of Historic Places.

Cooper River Bridges

SCOTT HENDERSON
CANON ELAN
VELVIA

When it opened in 1929, the Cooper River Bridge, officially titled the John P. Grace Memorial Bridge, was the fifth longest suspension bridge in the world. Seemingly ill-fated, the bridge took 14 workers' lives, 14 months to complete, and nearly six million dollars. In 1946 a freighter adrift in high winds plowed into the eastern section, tearing away the roadway and killing five. The second bridge, the Silas N. Pearman Bridge, was added in 1966.

Drayton Hall *(top)*

LISA THOMPSON
CANON ELAN 2E
FUJI 200
F11

Completed in 1742, Drayton Hall has been acclaimed as the finest early Georgian style house in America. Fashioned after an English manor house, Drayton Hall was owned by Royal Judge John Drayton, considered to be one of the wealthiest planters of Charleston colony.

Landscape at Drayton Hall *(bottom)*

TOMETTA O. JOHNSON
CANON REBEL 2000

Drayton Hall, unaltered since its building in 1742, survived the Civil War by serving as a smallpox hospital for freed slaves.

Johnny Jump-Ups

LUCY MARSHALL BAXTER
NIKON N50
KODAK 400
F22

Velvet petals of pansies bloom in the gardens at Middleton Place. With the help of his friend, the famed French botanist, Andre Michaux, Henry Middleton turned the gardens of Middleton plantation into a southern horticultural heaven.

Reflecting Waters at Middleton Place *(opposite)*

PAMELA ECCLES
MINOLTA MAXXUM 500 SL
FUJI

The gardens of Middleton Place were fashioned after the famous classical gardens of Europe. The precisely laid paths and ordered symmetry of one of the earliest examples of classical landscaped gardens in North America offer visitors alternating views of private outdoor spaces, reflecting ponds, and sweeping vistas of the Ashley River.

Boardwalk on Sullivan's Island *(left)*

C. CAROLYN THIEDKE
CANON SURE SHOT

Since the 19th century, Sullivan's Island has been a summer escape for Charlestonians seeking relief from the heat of the city.

Charles Towne Landing *(below)*

KRISTIN KIFER
OLYMPUS OM 2N
100 KODAK SLIDE
F16

Now a state park, Charles Towne Landing, the site of Charleston's first settlement in 1670, shows the lush beauty that beckoned the first settlers.

Man and Nature *(opposite)*

MELISSA M. FRASER
CANON EOS 650
KODAK GOLD 200
F5.6

Open to the public since 1870, the gardens of Magnolia Plantation are still owned and operated by descendants of the Drayton family. The gardens wind lazily through 390 acres of magnolia trees, azaleas, camellias, lakes and swamp gardens.

Dunes on the Isle of Palms

JENNIFER J. DALY
NIKON F620
KODAK 400
F8

Five miles long and barely 1/2 mile wide, the sandy coastal strip of land known as the Isle of Palms has long been an idyllic getaway for Carolinians of the Lowcountry.

US Coast Guard Lighthouse *(opposite)*

CHARLES E. REIST
PENTAX IQZOOM 80-E
FUJI 200

Charleston is a seagoing city with access to the Ashley and Cooper Rivers. Since its founding, it has been an extremely busy hub for fishing fleets, merchant vessels and naval ships.

Wetsuit

DEL SCHUTTE
OLYMPUS
KODAK 200 GOLD

Looking like a diminutive, latter day pirate, a young visitor on the Isle of Palms goes about the business of finding treasure.

The USS Yorktown *(above)*

CHARLES E. REIST
PENTAX IQZOOM 80-E
FUJI 200

The "Fighting Lady" of WWII, the aircraft carrier USS Yorktown was commissioned in 1943 and is the flagship of the Patriots Point Fleet in Charleston Harbor.

From the Bridge to the Isle of Palms *(left)*

BENJAMIN FINE
NIKON 70
KODAK MAX 400

South Carolina businessman J.C. Long, who owned the entire Isle of Palms, began selling lots for small vacation homes following World War II. Since then, the community has gained a distinct reputation as a fun island escape as well as a comfortable place to live year round.

Sullivan Island Lighthouse *(opposite)*

WILLIAM PALMER
NIKON N90S
FUJI PROVIA

Commissioned in 1962 to replace the aging Morris Island Lighthouse, the Charleston Light on Sullivan's Island, built with steel girders and aluminum panels, has office space at the bottom and top of the tower, necessitating both an elevator and air conditioning. Because it's original 28,000,000 candlepower light was so intense as to be dangerous, it was de-intensified in 1967 to 1,170,000 candlepower.

The Fighting Lady *(top)*

PHOTO COURTESY OF PATRIOTS POINT
NAVAL AND MARITIME MUSEUM

The USS Yorktown, "The Fighting Lady," commissioned in 1943, was named in honor of the first USS Yorktown sunk at Midway. This second Lady saw a great deal of action in the Pacific during WWII, receiving 11 battle stars for her service.

Go Navy *(bottom)*

PHOTO COURTESY OF PATRIOTS POINT
NAVAL AND MARITIME MUSEUM

After a few alterations and additions, the USS Yorktown was converted to carry jets in 1955. She served as an anti-submarine carrier in Vietnam and, before being decommissioned in 1970, she recovered the crew of Apollo 8 in 1968 after the historic spacecraft's return from the first manned mission to orbit the moon.

The USS Yorktown

The *USS Yorktown* continues to serve her nation as the National Memorial to Carrier Aviation, and Patriots Point offers a wide variety of exhibits about maritime and naval life and history. Within the complex are exhibits ranging from the Congressional Medal of Honor Society's museum and headquarters, a full-size Vietnam era Navy Advance Tactical Support Base, to exhibits on daily life aboard an aircraft carrier and memorials to carrier personnel killed in action.

Patriots Point *(above)*

PHOTO COURTESY OF PATRIOTS POINT
NAVAL AND MARITIME MUSEUM

Located in Mount Pleasant, directly across the harbor from the Charleston Peninsula, Patriots Point is an unusually large and diverse maritime museum. It is home to four permanently moored vessels, including the famous aircraft carrier, the USS Yorktown, and 25 vintage aircraft.

Submarine Clamagore *(left)*

PHOTO COURTESY OF PATRIOTS POINT
NAVAL AND MARITIME MUSEUM

Commissioned in the late stages of the war in the Pacific, the USS Clamagore was one of the last U.S. Navy's diesel powered submarines when she was decommissioned in 1975. Based mainly at Charleston during her 30 year career, she cruised the Atlantic and Mediterranean as well as the Caribbean waters during the critical moments of the Cuban missile crisis in 1962.

Fort Sumter

WILLIAM PALMER
NIKON N90S
FUJI PROVIA

Still possessing a powerful presence, Fort Sumter was the site of the first military action of the War Between the States. After declaring secession, Union forces were still stationed at Fort Sumter. After Northern troops refused official demands to surrender the fort, a mortar shell was fired over the fort from Fort Johnson on April 12th, 1861.

Sullivan's Island Beach and Lighthouse

DEBRA GINGRICH, CAROLINA HELICOPTER SERVICES, INC.
MINOLTA 3XI
FUJI 100
AUTO

Now a popular and peaceful residential island, it is difficult to remember that Sullivan's Island has a far richer, and often less idyllic history. It was the point of debarkation for thousands of imported slaves between 1700 and 1775. At the far northwestern tip of Sullivan's Island is Fort Moultrie, which was the stage for significant and symbolic moments in both the Revolutionary and Civil Wars. Edgar Allen Poe was stationed at Fort Moultrie as a young soldier, and which later inspired the story, "The Gold Bug," and the famous Seminole Indian chief, Osceola, was held prisoner at this notorious fort until his death.

Here on Sullivan's Island

DEBRA GINGRICH, CAROLINA HELICOPTER SERVICES, INC.
MINOLTA 3XI
FUJI 100
AUTO

It was Florentia O'Sullivan, Captain of the *Carolina,* who brought the first English settlers to the region, for whom Sullivan's Island was named. Only three miles long and less than a quarter mile wide, Sullivan's Island served as a strategic defense for settlers in the Low-country.

Historic Downtown

St. Michael's

JAMES BLANK
PENTAX 67
EKTACHROME 64
F16

The oldest church building in Charleston, St. Michael's has withstood severe tests of man and nature. During the Civil War, the steeple was painted black to make it less visible to Union gunners; an earthquake cracked the structure in 1886; tornadoes in 1935 and 1989 did their damage, as well as Hurricane Hugo in 1989.

46 Tradd Street

E. B. HESTON
HASSEL BLAD
AGFA VELVIA
F22

Constructed in 1770 by James Vanderhorst, this Georgian style home was bought sometime after 1919 by Alfred Hutty, a print maker from Woodstock, New York. Hutty was an early member of the Charleston Renaissance, a group of artists active in the city in the 1920's and '30's. His prints are still part of the Gibbes Art Museum collection. Creeping fig and other wall-covering plants were, in fact, an effective method of climate control in sunny South Carolina.

The Gates at 14 Lagare Street *(opposite)*

JAMES BLANK
PENTAX 67
EKTACHROME 64
F11

Built by successful John's Island planter, Francis Simmons in 1800, the house at 14 Lagare Street is a classic example of a Charleston single house. The ornate brick and wrought iron gates with the elaborately stone pinecones were put in place by the second owner, George Edwards in 1816.

St. Phillip's Church at Christmastide *(above)*

PATTEN J. DEW
CANON EOS 3
FUJI REALA

After the original 18th century edifice was destroyed by fire, the current church of St. Phillip's was designed in 1835 by Joseph Nyde. It was once called "the Lighthouse Church" because of the light that was put in the steeple to direct ships into the harbor.

East Battery Homes *(opposite)*

JAMES BLANK
PENTAX 67
EKTACHROME 64
F16

These homes on East Battery command a magnificent view of the waters of the Cooper River and the harbor.

Mansion on South Battery

JAMES BLANK
PENTAX 67
EKTACHROME 64
F16

The houses on South Battery are an eclectic mix of architectural styles
but all exhibit a soft grandeur that is distinctly Charleston.

Urban Gardens on South Battery *(opposite)*

JAMES BLANK
PENTAX 67
EKTACHROME 64
F22

Formal green spaces meet genteel urbanity at a home on South Battery.

Slave Mart Museum

JAMES BLANK
PENTAX 67
EKTACHROME 64
F22

The Old Slave Mart at 6 Chalmers Street was one of several places in
Charleston where slaves were bought and sold as early as 1856. The
museum, owned by the city of Charleston since 1988, has exhibits
which show not only the saga of slavery in America, but also African
and Caribbean culture, emancipation, the Reconstruction era and the
Civil Rights Movement.

Homes of South Battery *(opposite)*

JAMES BLANK
PENTAX 67
EKTACHROME 64
F16

The rise of cotton in the late 18th century as the South's biggest cash
crop brought the port city of Charleston a new era of wealth. Wealthy
planters and shipping merchants built opulent, fashionable townhouses
of the finest materials.

St. Philip's

CHRISTY HAGER
CANON EOS REBEL X
FUJICHROME 100

St. Philip's has played a vital role in the religious life of Charleston for more than 300 years. The classically inspired church was designed after the original building was destroyed by fire in1835.

Broad Street *(left)*

JAMES BLANK
LINHOF 4X5
EKTACHROME 64
F45

In 1931, the Charleston City Council designated 144 acres as an Historic District, creating the first American Historic City Government Ordinance. The Historic Charleston Foundation was established in 1947. The Foundation assisted in the Broad Street Beautification Program in 1968, and rehabilitation of the historic commercial district continues to the present.

Pillars and Pots *(above)*

BONNIE B. DORAZIO
MINOLTA X-370
KODACOLOR 100
F8

Charleston's graceful, old buildings are well supported both literally and figuratively. Charleston adopted America's first Historic City Government Ordinance in 1931. The Historic Charleston Foundation was formed in 1947. Buyers of old and historic properties can find support and help from the Resource Center of the Preservation Society of Charleston and other organizations.

Eastern Tiger Alighting *(right)*

AMY PURVIS
NIKON N60
FUJI
F11

A common glimpse of beauty in Lowcountry gardens, an Eastern Tiger Swallowtail butterfly alights on the brilliant petals of an autumn zinnia.

Harp Gate on Church Street

E. B. HESTON
HASSEL BLAD
AGFA VELVIA
F22

Charleston's distinctive wrought iron gates, fences, and window grates
were largely created by German smiths in the 18th and 19th centuries.
At one time, Charleston had more iron work than any other city in
America. Much of the handsomely wrought work, however, as well as
many of the city's church bells were sacrificed and melted down for the
Confederate Cause.

Wrought Iron and White Porches

JAMES BLANK
PENTAX 67
EKTACHROME 64
F11

Gorgeous wrought iron gates and cool, welcoming porches are distinctly part of Charleston architecture.

Isn't it Romantic? *(above)*

SARAH F. GOLDMAN
CANON AE-1
35MM 400
AUTO

Charleston's White Point Gardens, better known as The Battery, with its sweeping, mossy live oaks and Victorian gazebo gives an air of romantic southern charm. The area became widely used as a park around 1837, but the battery has been witness to over 300 years of Charleston's rich—and often violent—history.

Passage *(left)*

NICOLE REGINA WRONA
NIKON AF N6006
KODAK GOLD 100
F5.6

Charleston is a city full of little sidestreets, nooks and crannies, hidden quiet green spots and private passageways. This narrow, shadowed entryway off Broad Street leads on to some private delight beyond.

Gates on South Battery *(opposite)*

JAMES BLANK
PENTAX 67
EKTACHROME 64
F16

A graceful, moss-draped live oak shades the sidewalks of South Battery. Charleston's pedestrian-friendly streets invite visitors and residents alike to savor the city's distinctive architecture.

Edmondston-Alston House on East Bay Street

JAMES BLANK
PENTAX 67
EKTACHROME 64
F8

Charles Edmondston, a shipping merchant from Scotland, built a
Federal style house on East Bay Street in 1828. After Edmondston
lost his fortune in the cotton panic of 1837, the subsequent
owner, Charles Alston, renovated the structure into the stylish
Greek Revival townhouse that exists today.

The Palmer House, 5 East Battery *(top)*

CAROL GORDON
NIKON F3HP
KODAK GOLD
AUTO

Known as "The Pink Palace," this Italianate Charleston single house was built in 1849 by John Ravenel. Ravenel was a physician and scientist who invented phosphate fertilizer, the making of which became an economic lifeboat for Charleston during the lean years following the Civil War.

Piazza in Pink *(bottom)*

LARRY TOMSIC
OLYMPUS INFINITY SUPER ZOOM 300
KODAK GOLD 100
F11

French Roman Catholics, refugees from the slave uprisings in Haiti, settled in Charleston in the late 18th century. They brought their architectural ideas of breezy side galleries which became the much noted piazzas and brought fresh air to Charleston town homes. This gracious, pastel house near the battery has the distinctive broad side porches, tall windows and high ceilings for which Charleston homes are famous.

Charleston Spring

MELISSA M. FRASER
CANON EOS 650
KODAK ROYAL 200
F5.6

Spring comes early to Charleston, and the city fairly bursts with bloom-
ing azaleas, camellias and romantic, aromatic wisteria.

Bee Block on Bull Street

E. B. HESTON
HASSEL BLAD
AGFA VELVIA
F22

A row of Italianate style townhouses comprise Bee Block, named for a Charleston merchant who used them as shops during the War Between the States to sell merchandise that had eluded the blockade of the harbor. These townhouses were far enough north on the peninsula to be out of range of the shelling from the harbor.

Sunset Sails

COURTESY OF CHARLESTON AREA
CONVENTION AND VISITORS BUREAU

A sailboat glides past the Charleston battery.

Rainbow Row

Charleston's historic architecture, beautifully and lovingly preserved, is one of the city's greatest legacies.

Waterfront Park *(above)*

MICHAEL RONQUILLO
NIKON 8008S
FUJICHROME ASTIA 100
F5.6

One of Charleston's most popular parks, Waterfront Park, offers views
of the harbor and a place to cool off during sultry Carolina summers.

Porcher House *(opposite)*

E. B. HESTON
HASSEL BLAD
AGFA VELVIA
F22

Built in 1857 by Francis Porcher, a wealthy planter and a delegate to
the South Carolina Secession Convention, this pink Greek Revival
blended house later held the offices of a young naval lieutenant,
John F. Kennedy, during WWII. Currently the house is divided into
three separate condominiums.

SOS

GABRIELLA R. BROWN
CANON ELAN II EOS
KODAK 400

A sailing instructor at the Carolina Yacht Club comes to the aid of a boat of students that has capsized in the Charleston Harbor.

Hiking Out?

GABRIELLA R. BROWN
CANON ELAN II EOS
KODAK 400

Students of the Carolina Yacht Club sailing program scramble to right their boat as they round a mark in Charleston Harbor. Boats and boating are tightly woven to Lowcountry life. The Trident region, which includes Charleston and surrounding areas represents almost 13% of total registered boats in South Carolina.

Tallship and the Steeple of St. Michael's *(opposite)*

PATTEN J. DEW
CANON EOS3
FUJI REALA

Once bustling with ships of war, today Charleston Harbor is a lively port for every type of recreational and merchant vessel.

Ring Billed Gulls on the Battery

BENJAMIN J. PADGETT
NIKON N80
FUJI SUPERIA 400
F/8

The high-pitched cries of gulls wheeling over Charleston Harbor are part of the waterfront's background music.

Tall Ship in Charleston Harbor *(opposite)*

BRAD SCHWARTZ
NIKON 4004
KODAK MAX 400
F16

Taken from the bow of a tall ship, this photo gives another uniquely historic perspective on Charleston. Charleston's maritime history is a rich and diverse one, and celebrated by its citizenry. In particular, the South Carolina Maritime Heritage Foundation, a non-profit group founded by passionate maritime enthusiasts is spearheading the building of *The Spirit of South Carolina,* a tall ship fashioned after an historical Carolina schooner, which will be constructed near the Charleston aquarium.

Marching Music

MICHAEL RONQUILLO
NIKON 8008S
KODACHROME 64
F4

Street musicians on Charleston's downtown Market Street accompany Citadel cadets marching in formation.

Charleston Neighborhood *(opposite)*

JAMES BLANK
PENTAX 67

Charleston entered its first "Golden Age" around 1730, when shipping and trade made planters and merchants wealthy. The city's building industry burgeoned with new, stylish mansions that were periodically remodeled to keep pace with changing fashion. Consequently, Charleston's neighborhoods are a vibrant mix of architectural style and cool green space.

Rainbow Row *(top)*

DEBRA GINGRICH, CAROLINA HELICOPTER SERVICES, INC.
MINOLTA 3XI
FUJI 100
AUTO

These Georgian-style townhouses on East Bay street were built as offices and residences for cotton brokers and shipping merchants starting around 1740. Convenient to the Cooper River wharf, where the merchants' ships would dock, the area fell into decay in the late 19th century. In the early part of the 20th century, Susan Pringle Frost bought, restored, and sold one of these houses, thus starting the revival of preserving Charleston's historic buildings.

East Battery Homes Along the Cooper River *(bottom)*

DEBRA GINGRICH, CAROLINA HELICOPTER SERVICES, INC.
MINOLTA 3XI
FUJI 100
AUTO

Originally named Oyster Point due to the bleached white oyster shells that littered the beach, the south tip of the Charleston peninsula was mostly beach and tidal marsh. In the mid 19th century, however, seawalls were built and the land was filled in, creating some of Charleston's most desirable real estate.

Ships, Ships, and Tall Ships in Charleston Harbor

DEBRA GINGRICH, CAROLINA HELICOPTER SERVICES, INC.
MINOLTA 3XI
FUJI 100
AUTO

Propelled by a fine, northwesterly breeze, a tall ship joins a fleet of motorcraft and sailing boats on the Cooper River heading towards Charleston Harbor.

Colonial Lake

PATTEN J. DEW
CANON EOS3
FUJI REALA

Smack dab in the middle of an historic, downtown neighborhood, this
saltwater lake is a popular running spot, but also a pleasant fishing hole.

Dock Street Theater on Church Street

JAMES BLANK
PENTAX 67
EKTACHROME 64
F16

The Dock Street Theater, the oldest theatrical building still in use from colonial times, was rehabilitated in the 1930's under the New Deal's Work Project to give work to unemployed architects and craftsmen. The interior was rebuilt in the style of earlier Georgian theaters, seating 463 people in an old world setting. The theater itself, however, is capable of handling modern productions.

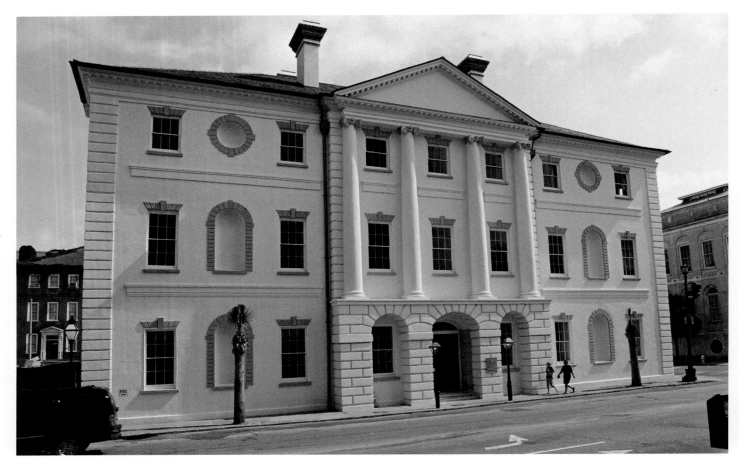

The Corner of Meeting Street and Broad:
The Court House at the Four Corners of Law

JOAN B. LUCAS
CANON EOS ELAN II
KODAK GOLD 200

Heavily damaged in 1989 by Hurricane Hugo, The Charleston
County Courthouse was renovated in 2001 to its 1792 condition.
The courthouse sits on the site of the old State Building, which was
gutted by fire in 1788. Found in the basement, during the recent
twelve million dollar renovation, were some old timbers which are
speculated to be from the original Charles Towne drawbridge.

Here is the Steeple *(opposite)*

MELISSA M. FRASER
CANON EOS 650
FUJI 400
F8

The eight bronze bells in the steeple of St. Michael's Episcopal Church
were cast in London in 1764. Since their first sounding on September
21st, 1764, these famous bells have made the trip back and forth to
England three times.

Grand Magnolia

J. KELLY CONDON
PENTAX
KODAK

An ancient species, native to much of North America, the plesantly-aromatic, plate-sized white blooms of the hardy magnolia have become an enduring symbol of the American south.

Widow's Weeds on May 10th: Confederate Memorial Day at Magnolia Cemetery

BONNIE B. DORAZIO
MINOLTA X-370
KODACOLOR 100
F8

"Remember, it is your duty to see that the true history of the South is presented to future generations."–Lt. General Stephen Dill Lee, United Confederate Veterans, 1906. Located on the banks of the Cooper River, 19th century Magnolia Cemetery is the final resting place for generations of Southern and Confederate Leaders.

Lush, Not Overgrown (opposite)

LARRY TOMSIC
OLYMPUS INFINITY SUPER ZOOM 300
KODAK GOLD 100
F11

The picturesque, un-manicured, lush graveyard of the Unitarian Church in Charleston is the beginning of the Gateway Walk, a self-guided walk through Charleston's hidden gardens and churchyards.

Window Boxes on King Street *(above)*

MELISSA M. FRASER
CANON EOS 650
KODAK GOLD 100
F5.6

Considered to be Charleston's Shopping Mecca, offering a range of shops from The Gap to Antique Row, King Street is actually a long street that begins far up on the peninsula and ends as a scenic, narrow passage through a charming collection of pre-Revolutionary private homes.

Broadus *(left)*

CAROL GORDON
NIKON N6006
KODAK
AUTO

A Gullah word for "something extra–at no charge," broadus might also include the contributions of the West African slaves that were brought to the Carolina Lowcountry and would be inextricably entwined in its complex history. Shipped to the region from West Africa via the West Indies, black slaves brought with them the knowledge of marsh cultivation of rice, a South Carolina staple, both as an export commodity and on the Lowcountry table. Sweetgrass weavers still make fanner baskets identical to the ones their ancestors used to separate rice from the chaff in the rice growing areas of West Africa.

Sweetgrass on Broad

BONNIE B. DORAZIO
MINOLTA X-370
KODACOLOR 100
F8

Handmade with bunches of sweetgrass, pine needles, and bullrush and bound with fibers of native palmetto, sweetgrass basket weaving is a traditional African-American craft of the Lowcountry since the early 1700's. Celebrated in museums from New York, to Rome, these uniquely Lowcountry art pieces can be bought on the sidewalks of Charleston's streets and rural highways.

Barn Doors After the Horses

KARIN M. SMITH
NIKON F100
EKTACHROME 200
F11

Even old barns reap the benefits of Charleston's love affair with its historic architecture. Here a gracious old brick carriage house has been renovated for modern purposes.

The Old Jail

JENNIFER J. DALY
NIKON F620
AGFA OPTIMA 200
F5.6

Built in 1802, this decaying building served as the municipal jail until 1939. The main building was for whites only; the slave workhouse, since torn down, was on the same block. The gallows also remained standing here until Hurricane Hugo washed it away in 1989.

Too Poor to Paint, Too Proud to Whitewash *(opposite)*

PAMELA ECCLES
CANON AT 1
FUJI

During the Reconstruction period following the Civil War, Charlestonians were too poor and too exhausted to reconstruct their city, but southern pride gave rise to the saying: "too poor to paint, too proud to whitewash." As a fortuitous result of these hard times, most of Charleston's distinctive buildings were saved from indiscriminate demolition and survived to be lovingly restored.

Painted Lady *(above)*

DIANA HOLLINGSWORTH GESSLER
MINOLTA 140 EX
FUJI 200

Even though they have survived war, hurricanes, earthquakes, cyclones and hard times, Charleston's old wood houses still require a great deal of TLC. This Georgian *grande dame* at 64 South Battery is getting a little facelift and cosmetic touch up.

8 Lagare Street *(left)*

BENJAMIN J. PADGETT
CANON ELAN IIE
KODAK GOLD 400
F16

Charlestonians have their own pronunciations for their city's streets. If you stop and ask directions for "Legare Street," you probably won't find it; ask for "La-GREE Street" though, and you'll happily find yourself strolling past the Cleland-Kinlock-Huger house, built in 1857. In the early 20th century, the Italianate house became the residence of Burnett Rhett Maybank, one-time mayor of Charleston, then Governor of South Carolina, and finally a US senator.

Building and Oak on the College of Charleston Campus *(opposite)*

LARRY TOMSIC
OLYMPUS INFINITY SUPER ZOOM 300
KODAK GOLD 100
F11

As the oldest municipal college in the U.S., the College of Charleston occupies over 100 buildings in the heart of the city's historic downtown.

Windows on Chalmers Street

PAMELA ECCLES
FUJI

Looking much as it did 200 years ago when it was the city's notorious
red light district, Chalmers Street is Charleston's longest stretch of cob-
blestone street. Stucco was also a common building material in the
region. Due to the sandy, porous quality of local bricks, stucco was used
to seal walls against the elements.

Spring Bursts Forth at Trinity United Methodist Church *(above)*

BENJAMIN J. PADGETT
NIKON N80
KODAK GOLD 400
F16

Religious freedom attracted many different religious faiths, earning Charleston the nickname: "The Holy City." Although the colony had been founded by English settlers, French Huguenots, Congregationalists, Presbyterians, Jews, Lutherans, Methodists and Catholics all practiced their religions freely, building dozens of churches in the 18th and 19th century in a wide variety of architectural styles.

The Pineapple Fountain *(right)*

KARIN M. SMITH
NIKON F100
EKTACHROME 200

Brought back from tropical travels by ship merchants, the pineapple became a symbol of hospitality and welcome. Located in Waterfront Park, near the cruise ship terminal, this giant pineapple offers visitors coming ashore a refreshing welcome.

The Gate of the College of Charleston, 66 George Street

SOPHIE HELTAI
OLYMPUS SUPER ZOOM
KODAK
AUTO/FLASH

The main gate to the College of Charleston has seen more than 150 years of the state's oldest college history. It was built in 1850 by local architect, Col. Edward Brickle White who was also the designer of St. Phillip's Church Steeple, the Huguenot Church, and Market Hall.

Tribute to Washington *(opposite)*

RONALD GORDON
MINOLTA 7000 MAXXUM
KODAK
AUTO

A bronze statue of the American father stands in Washington Park, named after Washington's victory at Yorktown. The statue, funded in part by General William Westmoreland, was done by Charleston Artist, John Michel.

Perspective with Plants *(above)*

SARAH F. GOLDMAN
CANON AE-1
35 MM 400
AUTO

A shady, breezy piazza invites passersby to take a refreshing peek. These long, cool, often multi-story porches, which run along the entire side of Charleston houses, made a dramatic difference to summer living in the steamy Lowcountry.

Cobblestones *(left)*

CYNTHIA WATERLANDER
PENTAX

The cobblestones that make up Charleston's famously charming streets arrived in the city in the holds of merchant ships. Once in harbor, the stone ballast was unloaded and replaced by cotton, indigo and rice for transport back to Europe.

Waterfront Park

CYNTHIA WATERLANDER
PENTAX

After developers in the 1970's unveiled a plan to develop this last stretch of Charleston waterfront property into high-rise residential and commercial buildings, the city acquired the property for Waterfront Park in 1979 with private funds and a matching Federal grant. This 12-acre park along the Cooper River waterfront, which cost nearly $13.5 million dollars to design and build, was ravaged by Hurricane Hugo before it was complete. With characteristic Charlestonian determination however, the pieces were picked up and the project was completed on time.

One Horse Open Sightseeing Buggy

CAROL GORDON
NIKON F3HP
KODAK GOLD
AUTO

Charleston's quaint historic streets, mild weather, and relaxed pace, even during the hectic holiday season, make sightseeing in an open carriage ideal.

Poinsettias and Green Ivy

CAROL GORDON
NIKON F3HP
KODAK GOLD
AUTO

Charleston has a warm, humid climate. Christmases are often green, outdoor affairs, even when there's a nip in the subtropical air.

Unitarian Church and Churchyard *(opposite)*

JENNIFER J. DALY
NIKON F620
AGFA OPTIMA 200

Originally built as an expansion for the Meeting Street Independent Church, this church building was rechartered as the Unitarian Church in Charleston in 1839. Nearly completed at the beginning of the Revolutionary War, the church was used as barracks for British militia. British horses were stabled in the sanctuary.

Citadel Cadet

COURTESY OF RUSS PAGE, CITADEL PHOTOGRAPHER
DIGITAL

A Citadel cadet stands at the front gate to The Citadel. The college was all-male until 1996 when it opened to women. Five years later, nearly 100 women have become members of the Corps of Cadets.

Military Dress *(left)*

COURTESY OF RUSS PAGE, CITADEL PHOTOGRAPHER
DIGITAL

Symmetry and precision mark the military dress parades at The Citadel. The parades, which are held most Friday afternoons when the college is in session, draw thousands of visitors each year.

Parade on the Quadrangle

Citadel cadets get into formation for the weekly military parades on the red and white quadrangle in the barracks. The parades, which take place most Friday afternoons when the college is in session, are free and open to the public.

Corps of Cadets Guard *(right)*

Cadets march in a parade at The Citadel with Summerall Chapel in the background. Spiritual reflection and adherence to an honor code are important components of life in the Corps of Cadets.

South to Kiawah Island

Folly Beach Pier: A Thousand Feet
from the Edge of America

CHARLES BONDO
PENTAX K1000
FUJI SUPER HQ 200
F5.6

Folly Beach has given itself the nickname,
"The Edge of America." The Pier, which
was built in the 1930's, drew big name performers and big crowds. Destroyed by fire
in 1957 and again in 1977, the new fishing
pier was finished in 1995 and is still a
landmark for pleasure seekers from
Charleston and beyond.

Clean the Decks

SARAH F. GOLDMAN
CANNON AE1
35MM 400
AUTO

A fisherman cleans his boat at Crosby's Fish and Shrimp Company.

Boats on James Island *(opposite)*

BRAD SCHWARTZ
NIKON 4004
KODAK MAX 400
F16

New roads connecting the rural James Island to the Charleston Peninsula have been a catalyst for real estate development. Commercial shrimp boats and pleasure craft on lazy waters belie the rapid changes overcoming this once largely agricultural island.

In the Old Rice Fields

BENJAMIN FINE
NIKON 70
KODAK MAX 400
F4

An egret wends his way through the waters of an old rice marsh in Ravenel. It was the cultivation of rice that made the fortunes of Charleston planters and it was the labor-intensive growing of rice that necessitated the constant influx of slave labor. Now abandoned, these old rice fields have succumbed to the natural ebbs and flows of Lowcountry life.

Beached *(opposite)*

ELISABETH FANCY HILL
NIKON PRONEAS
SEATTLE FILMWORKS
F5.8

The silent, sinuous canoe is an ideal way to explore South Carolina's endless waterways, rivers, ponds and marshes. Home to bird life, alligators, manatees and fish, Carolina waters are an integral part of the Lowcountry experience.

Morris Island Lighthouse

E. B. HESTON
HASSEL BLAD
AGFA VELVIA

The 161 foot high lighthouse was once surrounded by land and a three story Victorian mansion which housed the lighthouse keeper, his two assistants and their families, and fourteen other buildings, which included a schoolhouse. The lighthouse survived devastating hurricanes and an earthquake, but has succumbed to time and erosion. Although efforts are being made to preserve the Morris Island Lighthouse, a new, modern lighthouse on nearby Sullivan's Island now has its job.

Sunrise on Kiawah Island

JULIE SCHNEIDER
NIKON LITE-TOUCH ZOOM
FUJI SUPER HG 200

Named after the tribe that inhabited this peaceful strip of land just west of James Island in the 16th to the 18th centuries, in 1739 Kiawah Island became first an indigo, then a cotton plantation for 246 years. In 1974, the Island grew a new crop: luxury homes, tennis courts and golf courses for a prestigious resort and residential community.

Ashley River

SUSAN P. SHAMOUN
MINOLTA X700
KODAK ELITECHROME 100
F5.6

Originally named the Kiawah river by local tribes, early English colonists promptly retitled the river the Ashley, in honor of one of the founding Lords Proprietors, the First Earl of Shaftesbury, Anthony Ashley Cooper.

Low Formation over Folly Beach *(top)*

KRISTINE KIFER
OLYMPUS OM2N
KODAK 100
F22

The diminutive barrier island of Folly Beach served as summering grounds for a tribe of Cussabee Indians up until the 17th century. The tribe disappeared from the Carolina Lowcountry by 1750.

Jetty at Folly Beach *(bottom)*

KRISTINE KIFER
OLYMPUS OM2N
KODAK 100
F5.6

Six miles long and barely a half mile wide, Folly Beach is a shifting, sandy strip of a barrier island that has witnessed violent conflict, creative inspiration, and lighthearted pursuit of pleasure.

Ashley River Bridge

SUSAN P. SHAMOUN
MINOLTA X-700
KODAK ELITECHROME 100
F22

The antiquated and famously congested bridges that cross the Ashley
River to the Charleston peninsula still open to allow boats passage.

West Ashley

ALLENE C. BARANS
CANON ELON
KODAK
F6.7

The site of Charleston's first shopping mall and first postwar subdivision, West Ashley—the neighborhood west of peninsular Charleston and across the Ashley River is Charleston's economic corridor.

A High View of the Lowcountry

ALLENE C. BARANS
CANON ELON
KODAK
F6.7

An aerial view of nightfall on the Ashley River.

Up a Lazy River

DONNA HUFFMAN
NIKON 2020
EKTACHROME
F11

Sultry sunset on a lazy, Lowcountry river.

Sunrise on Folly Beach *(following page)*

WILLIAM PALMER
NIKON N90S
FUJI PROVIA

During the war between the states, Union batteries capped both ends of this small slip of a barrier island and garrisoned thousands of Union soldiers. Folly Beach eventually overcame its war torn past to become a quaint, relaxed vacation spot.

Folly Beach

CHARLES E. REIST
PENTAX IQZOOM 80-E
FUJI 200

The population of the Island of Folly Beach registers somewhere around 1600. During the sweltering summer days, however, the number triples as visitors flock to its long wide stretches of white sand beaches.

Tides Toll on a Solitary Beacon–Morris Island Lighthouse *(opposite)*

BILLIE JO COLE
PENTEX 70IQ ZOOM
KODAK 200

Morris Island Lighthouse Station at the entrance to Charleston Harbor was established in 1767. The current conical structure of dressed stone was built in 1876 and was deactivated in 1962.

Folly Beach Pier

PATTEN J. DEW
EOS3 CANON
FUJI NFH400

Part Gershwin, part Gidget, the style of the Edwin S. Taylor Fishing Pier at Folly Beach brings to mind both the classic, swinging times when George Gershwin lived at this quaint beach community, writing his opera, Porgy and Bess, and the unbridled fun of surfers in the 1950's and '60's when the Shag became South Carolina' official dance.

Jetty *(opposite)*

MICHAEL EMERICH
CANON REBEL G
FUJI
F5.6

Folly Beach has the most waterfront footage of any of the barrier islands that surround Charleston Harbor. But the actual numbers keep changing. Subject to Atlantic weather and tides, Folly Beach suffers the constant erosion of every barrier island. Jetties and beach renourishment programs attempt to keep the island from being swept away.

Summer Sunset, High Tide

MICHAEL EMERICH
CANON REBEL G
FUJI
F8

June 21st on the Folly River at Folly Beach County Park. Folly Beach
claims the honor of having set aside more public park acreage than any
other residential island in South Carolina.

Folly Beach Pier

CHARLES F. BONDO
PENTAX K1000
FUJI SUPER HQ 200
F5.6

Folly Beach Pier has been a magnet for fun seekers since the 1930's. The waves below attracted crowds of surfers. Performers such as Tommy Dorsey, Guy Lombardo, and the Ink Spots attracted crowds above.

Canoe Rest

DISNEY LEGEND
AL KONETZNI
OLYMPIA
KODAK 100

Sandlappers, a term used to describe the people of the Carolina Lowcountry, have lived a watery life for three hundred years. Twining black rivers, silent blackwater swamps and marshes that swell and ebb with the rhythm of the tides, are all a part of this life.

Cypress Swamp, Caw Caw Interpretive Center, Ravenel,
South Carolina.

JERRY L. SHELTON
MINOLTA MAX 7000
KODAK 100
AUTO

A stand of cypress wades in the black waters of Caw Caw Interpretive
Center, a 654 acre county park, near John's Island. The three counties
surrounding modern Charleston consist of over five hundred thousand
acres of wetlands, from rivers, blackwater swamps, and salt marshes to
ponds, lakes, and old rice fields.

Azaleas and Spanish Moss, Wadmalaw Island *(opposite)*

BONNIE B. DORAZIO
MINOLTA X-370
KODACOLOR 100
F11

Rural Wadmalaw Island, twenty miles south of Charleston is still largely
agricultural and is home to North America's only tea plantation. Tea,
South Carolina's official hospitality beverage, has actually been grown in
the Lowcountry since around 1799. It may have been accidentally
brought over with some other plant specimens by the botanist, Andre
Michaux, famous for introducing azaleas to the Carolinas.

Blood Horse

MERI BARRIOZ
F100 NIKON
400
F8

An Arabian Horse yearling at a farm in Hollywood, South Carolina, is a hot-blooded testament to South Carolina's enduring devotion to the culture of the horse. Wealthy genteel planters and merchants of Charleston and the Lowcountry regularly indulged their passion for hunting, horseracing, steeplechasing and other equestrian sport, a tradition that continues today.

He That Believeth Shall Not Make Haste *(opposite)*

SOPHIE HELTAI
OLYMPUS SUPER ZOOM
KODAK
AUTO

A bridge and still pond offer a moment's reflection beside the cemetery of Old St. Andrew's Church on Ashley River Road.

Lowcountry Walk

J. KELLY CONDON
PENTAX
KODAK GOLD

The Carolina Lowcountry is an intersection of daunting wilderness and
hospitable beauty.

Angel Oak, St. John's Island

E. B. HESTON
HASSEL BLAD
AGFA VELVIA
F22

Although live oak trees are native to the Carolina Lowcountry and are particularly common on the coastal islands, the gnarled majestic Angel Oak has survived 1400 years of hurricanes, fire, shipbuilding harvests, and war to become a living, awe inspiring monument in itself.

Folly Beach and Pier

DEBRA GINGRICH, CAROLINA HELICOPTER SERVICES, INC.
MINOLTA 3XI
FUJI 100
AUTO

Considered by many to be the Lowcountry's funkiest and most charming barrier island, Folly Beach is feeling the pressure to develop and "condo-ize."

Beacon to Forgotten History *(opposite)*

DEBRA GINGRICH, CAROLINA HELICOPTER SERVICES, INC.
MINOLTA 3XI
FUJI 100
AUTO

The Morris Island Lighthouse stands alone surrounded by water. During the Civil War, the original lighthouse was destroyed during the fierce battle for Battery Wagner. It was during that battle that Sgt. William Carney became the first black American soldier to receive the Congressional Medal of Honor. The present 1874 lighthouse fell victim to erosion, due to the construction of jetties on the island.

Allene C. Barans
644 Clearview Dr
Charleston, SC 29412
14, 18, 20, 107, 108

Meri Barrioz
P.O. Box 1075
Central, SC 29630
123

Lucy Marshall Baxter
124C Logan St.
Charleston, SC 29401
28

James Blank
1110 Red Maple Dr.
Chula Vista, CA 91910
back cover, 9, 20–21, 23, 24, 25,
42–43, 45, 46–47, 48, 49, 50,
51, 52, 55, 57, 58–59, 70–71,
75

Charles Bondo
1008 Riverhaven Circle Apt. R
Charleston, SC 29412
96–97, 117

Gabriella R. Brown
12 Water St.
Charleston, SC 29401
66 (2)

Billie Jo Cole
2551 Midland Pk. Rd. Lot 95
Charleston, SC 29406
113

J. Kelly Condon
1554 Downing St.
Charleston, SC 29407
78, 124

Jennifer J. Daly
1640 Baltusrol Ln.
Mt. Pleasant, SC 29466
32, 82, 93

Patten J. Dew
1035 Grand Concourse
Charleston, SC 29412
5, 47, 67, 74, 114

Bonnie B. Dorazio
2651 Oregon
Charleston, SC 29405
53, 78, 81, 120–121

Pamela Eccles
P.O. Box 21681
Charleston, SC 29413
29, 83, 86

Michael Emerich
P.O.Box 951
Folly Beach, SC 29439
115, 116

Benjamin Fine
424 Wappoo Rd
Charleston, SC 29407
34, 100

Melissa M. Fraser
1536 Inland Ave. Apt. C
Charleston, SC 29412
31, 60, 77, 80

Diana Hollingsworth Gessler
4140 Bayhead Dr. # 205
Bonita Springs, FL 34134
84

Sarah F. Goldman
9346 Circle Dr. East
Pinkerington, OH 43147
56, 90, 98

Carol Gordon
530 Oak bay Drive
Osprey, FL 34229
59, 80, 92(2)

Ronald Gordon
530 Oak Bay Drive
Osprey, FL 34229
89

Christy Hager
1 Besquet Ct. Apt. J1
Summerville, SC 29485
52

Sophie Heltai
2340-3 Treescape Dr
Charleston, SC 29414
22, 88, 122–123

Scott Henderson
529 Mill St.
Mt. Pleasant, SC 29464
26

E. B. Heston
P.O. Box 558
Ravenel, SC 29470
front cover, back cover, 10–11,
12–13, 44, 54, 61, 65, 102, 125

Elisabeth Fancy Hill
24 East Liberty St
Savannah, GA 31401
3, 101

Donna Huffman
P.O.Box 23754
Hilton Head Island, SC 29925
19, 109

Tometta O. Johnson
1593 Hamlin Rd.
Mt. Pleasant, SC 29466
27

Kristin Kifer
1421 Joy Ave.
Charleston, SC 29407
30, 105(2)

Al Konetzni
4934 Peridia Blvd. E.
Bradenton, FL 34203
118–119

Craig M. Lloyd
2329 Waring Hall Lane
Charleston, SC 29414
16

Joan B. Lucas
27.5 Wentworth St
Charleston, SC 29401
76

Benjamin J. Padgett
507 Cecilia Cove Drive
Charleston, SC 29412
68, 84, 87

William Palmer
2157 Stoneeood Dr
Charleston, SC 29412
6–7, 35, 39, 59, 110–111

Amy Purvis
P.O. Box 33
Highfalls, NC 27259
53

Charles E. Reist
1613 Livingstone St.
Sarasota, FL 34231
33, 34, 112

Michael Ronquillo
150 Leeward loop
Columbia, SC 29209
64, 70

Julie G. Rowe
1136 Old Course Lane
Mt. Pleasant, SC 29466
14, 15, 17

Julie Schneider
6618 Dogwood Ct
Fort Wayne, IN 46804
3, 103

Del Schutte
2700 Governors Pt. Ct.
Mt. Pleasant, SC 29466
32

Brad Schwartz
1752 Deer Path
Mt. Pleasant, SC29464
69, 99

Susan P. Shamoun
831 Toler Drive
Mt. Pleasant, SC 29464
16, 104, 106

Jerry L. Shelton
1 Whitetail Lane
Hague, NY 12836
120

Karin M. Smith
1630 HighlandFarm Dr.
Suwanee, GA 30024
82, 87

C. Carolyn Thiedke
P. O. Box 747
Sullivan's Island, SC 29482
30

Lisa Thompson
2274 Ashley River Rd # 602
Charleston, SC 29414
27

P. L. Tompkins
4465 Downing Place Way
Mt. Pleasant, SC 29466
22

Larry Tomsic
7168 Mill Run Circle
Naples, FL 34109
59, 79, 85

Cynthia Waterlander
141 Spooner Ct.
Goose Creek, SC 29445
90, 91

Nicole Regina Wrona
107 E. Waldburg St
Savannah, GA 31401
56